WORN

Adrienne Christian

sfwp.com

Library of Congress Cataloging-in-Publication Data

Names: Christian, Adrienne
Title: Worn / Adrienne Christian.
Description: Santa Fe, NM : SFWP (Santa Fe Writers Project), [2021] |
    Summary: "Using characters doubled over with grief, fear, and desire,
    the love poems in Worn mirror a photo album of legends, rumors, and
    memories exchanged over drinks in the early evening. Tenderness meets
    pain meets joy here, offering up the voices of Black folks fostering
    connection with their children, their lovers, and themselves.
    Christian's third collection of poetry takes the reader through love and
    longing, and manifests how we all cope and get dressed again after the
    harsh reality of our world lays us bare. From ghazals about erotic kinks
    to the disappointment of a father, these poems explore the clothes we
    reach for first when loss strips us naked"—Provided by publisher.
Identifiers: LCCN 2020039466 (print) | LCCN 2020039467 (ebook) | ISBN
    9781951631093 (trade paperback) | ISBN 9781951631109 (ebook)
Subjects: LCGFT: Poetry.
Classification: LCC PS3603.H74557 W67 2021 (print) |
    LCC PS3603.H74557 (ebook) | DDC 811/.6—dc23
LC record available at https://lccn.loc.gov/2020039466
LC ebook record available at https://lccn.loc.gov/2020039467

Published by SFWP
369 Montezuma Ave. #350
Santa Fe, NM 87501
(505) 428-9045
www.sfwp.com

For Monica

Contents

I.

How to Survive When You're the Only Black in the Office

or,

The New H.N.I.C.

One

morning, Uncle Steve was just ironing his shirt for work
when he started weeping.
First he bent at the waist and put his forehead on the ironing
board. Then his knees pulled him down to the floor.
He just folded—
all the way down
like a sitting giraffe.
Or, all the way down
like a shot giraffe.

January second.

Wedding Dress

Problem is, I need to be blotted out—
my family's DNA.
My daddy the gangster; his mother, the moron.
My mother, the daughter pimper; her mother, the monster.
When I finally met my mother's father,
and asked how many kids he had,
He spit, "What kinda dog go diggin around for shit?"
(My mother's mom was his coworker's wife.)
I asked my daddy if he was sure *sure* I was his firstborn
And he told me emphatically, "I think so. I'm pretty sure you are."
His daddy let him use his house to bring his women.
Even on Christmas—yes, I distinctly remember one
Christmas with young "Auntie Deb" smiling, unwrapping her shit
while my stepmom sat on the basement stairs crying in her eggnog.
A few of Daddy's prettiest cousins, he'd fucked, he admitted.
And when I met Uncle Womack's fresh-out-of-the-halfway-house son,
he said, "C'mon cuz, you want somethin to eat?"
He poured us beer and Cheetos on a plastic plate. As we ate,
he turned on a porno.
I told him, "No! Take me home! Now!"
I told my uncle and my dad. They asked,
"What were you wearing? Those jeans with the holes in the ass?"
This same uncle sold t-shirts at my half-sister's wedding:
This Ain't Swag—I'm Sick and Sore. And,
Dog is God Spelled Backwards.
Half the Hendrix have what they call The Sugar—
Long gone kidneys and toes, still making pies and drinking.
Uncle Kevin gave my daddy a kidney.
Daddy still drank and smoked in front of him.
I chose The Justice of the Peace to wed
because I know
my people aren't worth their $25 a plate—
I'd get $5 in a card from eight of them.
My Auntie Sally thought I was "marrying rich,"
because my fiancé had a business card.

Or as she called it, a bitniss card.
She wears every piece of jewelry she owns every single day.
All of it worth about thirteen dollars.
But for some reason, my man decides to marry me.
He keeps looking at me and can't stop smiling.
"Do you solemnly swear you are not brother and sister?"
the judge asked that day in January.
Both of us raised our hands. "We solemnly swear."
My new husband takes me home and while he's spewing semen inside me,
says, "I want to give you a baby."
But I'd already gone to my Nawlins aunties,
and gotten myself fixed
to not have kids
and not told him.
Yes, I knew he'd really wanted to have a family with me.
I also knew he didn't know what he was asking.

Estate Sale

Bree's grandmother had finally died.
She was a wreck. So I came to help.

I cooked. Cleaned.
I called and made arrangements with the folks
who would do Ms. Esther's estate sale.

The man from Capital Estate Services
came with his calculator
saying what was worth what
and why.

All Bree could do was lie on the floor and cry.
She said just one thing,
she wanted to keep her grandmother's emerald ring
to give to the woman who always drove her to church,
Ms. Mamie.

Then is when the fat man started to sweat.
"Oh, don't," he cried, pulling it out of her hand,
placing it back on the display.
He turned to me and mouthed, "Please tell
your friend she should never give away
something she can sell."

That was my mother's advice to me
on prom night:
Don't give away nuthin you can sell.
Now there were two of us
face down
on the floor,
as the man went about, doing his business.

Lincoln

The day I moved to Nebraska,
one of the states that voted in 45,
I took my dog out to tinkle
and my older, white, male neighbor
started chatting me up.

After "Hello" to me and "Hey there, shorty" to Bruiser:
"Ya know
I used to have a colored girl like you.
Same size and everything.
If you got a minute I'll run in n get a photograph n show you."

Colored.

I didn't want to be shown his fucking photograph.
(But I know better than to fall out with a neighbor.)
And he was an older man—
and my rule is never tell off old folks, even if they are old fools.
So, I waited while he rummaged.

And there on the photo was this *fabulous* Black lady,
looking like one of my aunties!
Velma-from-Good Times fro,
tight, high-waisted jeans,
halter top with her golden shoulders glowing bronze,

vaselined lips lined with brown pencil.
This could be one of the pictures on my mother's mantle!
Next to her, young him.
With them, two beige little snaggletooth cuties clutching wooden
trains.

He lifted his shirt sleeve
to show off his tat.
That's when I learned
the lady's name—
Rosetta.

Portrait of Everyone's Nana

That Christmas tree at Rockefeller Plaza.
Reminds me of my Auntie Song.

It's shaped like her.
Bright like her too.

Her house would also always smell like Pine
Sol. And she kept the Christmas lights up year-round.

On Christmas,
this woman would get *so* many presents,

she'd have to ask the givers to take them back,
hold on to them for her till next year please.

Right now, so many gifts
she couldn't walk.

She was all the neighbors' Auntie Song.
We all called her Auntie Song

because one *morsel* of anything she'd baked for you,
you would start dancing in your chair

at her little kitchen table.
Your legs would become those Rockettes'.

Your grown ass would end up seated up
on Auntie Song's big lap.

Wrapped in her housecoat
with the umbrellas on it.

Telling her everything
that had ever happened.

II.

How to Make a Sunday Chicken-Frying Dress

Go on, bow out. You won't soon forget the magic you made in this world, in your long red cotton blend strapless summer dress (Though some would call it a *gown.*). A stranger on the train asks which actress you are. Another asks if you are the devil. He said, *Smilin. Red. Attractive. That tail. Yeah, you gotsta to be the devil.* Facebook gave it more than four hundred comments, likes.

But like an old soldier in fatigues, having done his duty to Country, go on and lay it down now. Wash it. Dry it. On Heavy, in hot water. Stretch it out when it shrinks. Get it threadbare. Not so your nipples can show, so they *are* the show. Now get that ass in the kitchen. Fry a platter full of chicken. You hear that popping-grease sound? That's applause. You hear your man fold up his newspaper, having gotten a whiff. Here he comes to harass and kiss.

B. L. Z. R. D. 2 0 1 4

This morning's blizzard spells *Cup o' Noodles* in pajamas
playing *Love-And-Sex-Words-Only Scrabble.*

My sweetheart in a robe. All that chest hair showing.
Thigh and calve muscles like trucks in socks

smoking his cigar. It's my own turquoise robe my sweets is wearing.

I'd flung noodle juice on his robe when I'd caught his butt cheating!!—
hiding Zs and a Q in the pockets.

Plus, I'd grown too warm with the fireplace, heater, and hot tea with
whiskey and lemon.

Anyhoo, here we are now, making love with little letters,
after having made love all morning.

```
        F O R E V E R      S H O W M E
G L O E            I      E       O
O                  N      X       W
O                  G R I N        M
D                                 E
```

Note: We were allowed to spell words phonetically.

Soldier of Love

All those winters I spent in Michigan,
coddled by my car,
I could have been here
in Harlem.

Out walking in the snow,
only my own boots
on the ground.
Oh, glorious Outside.

Snow falling,
soft as jewelry box songs,
inspiring me into spinning,
arms up like a jewelry box girl.

All those years I spent in the car.
I could have been out here walking.
Sculpting my booty with every heavy trudge.
Toning my thighs with every lift and lay of each leg.

Up. Down. Left. Right. Forward. Home.
Getting home, getting my key from my bra.
Walking up all the steps to my place.
On the staircase,

turning to see a handsome man.
Seeing he had been following me!
Like the rats, he'd run in when I'd opened the door.
Little naughty thing trying to get warm.

Portrait of My Taurus Lover, Who Only Ever Wore Khakis, Wife Beaters, Flip Flops, and Yankee Fitteds

Walking to the Riverside Drive Fireworks.
We drink our way down to the eats—
dogs and burgers with
taters and maters. With
my head on his shoulder.
His hat on my head.
Henny in our red Solo cup.
Together.

Portrait of My Very Jealous Husband

No. What Adrienne loves is books.
For breakfast, it's tea, toast, watermelon, books.

In her bathroom on the sink, on every space around the tub,
it's bubble baths, sugar scrubs, magazines, books.

In her ponytail,
chewed No. 2s for marking books.

On her face. On her breasts. On her belly. In her little black
dresses' pockets, everywhere I look at my lady, books.

Forget going to the mall trying to buy this woman *anything*
other than the *only* thing she ever wants—books.

Have an argument, lose. Whatever you think you know, naw.
She already read the book on it. She already wrote the book

on it. No seeing me pull up, rushing out to take my bag. She's in the
window, yes. The window *seat*. Hugged up with a book.

I gotta wait on my mimosa and chicken n waffles on Sundays.
Belly *howling*. She's still in the goddamn bed with her book.

Been traveling two weeks. Get home, go lie down.
On *my* side of the bed, her dog and all her books.

Been busting through my boxers all night. Try to touch her,
she holds up a finger. "Almost finished with this book."

III.

Me Too?

Does having a man go through your panty drawer count?
My former landlord used to go through my panty drawer.

Mr. Nolte. He'd do repairs when I wasn't there. Then leave a jokey note:
Don't worry, I didn't root through your panty drawer.

Hahaha. Smiley face. It was always the same note –
I fixed X. And don't worry, I didn't go through your panty drawer.

Or, he'd leave a voicemail. *Nolte here. Took care of the wasp nest. And, don't worry—I didn't root through your panty drawer.*

I could tell my panties had been touched. But he never did anything too creepy like jerk off in my panty drawer.

So I'm wondering if this counts, if the only thing he did was root through my panty drawer.

The Boys in Blue

A Black woman's saving grace:

If ever he treats her wrong,
she can sock a Black man in his mouth.
She can bash in the motherfucker's car.
She can take his cash;
she can take his kids.
She can fuck his father;
she can fuck his friend.
She can spit in, and get all up in his face like this:
Do something, Boo; I dare you.
Because even if he so much as pushes her off,
she can call up the cops.
If *ever* that man does something to hurt her.
She can call the cops and prolly get him murdered.

neighborhood legend

for six long months
they lived by a bully

once he pinched her ass
when she walked past

sure she sent over her man
but the bully and his friends

were too much for one man
he went back to his porch

that man didn't speak
for three days

when she asked him which he wanted
pancakes or eggs

he just shook his head
no

but then he went knocking on folks' doors
two neighborhood legends' doors

the one who'd shot a police during the riots
and the one ran the center

they beat that poor kid till his teeth were chicklets
in their knuckles' gristles

we should run! the woman said when he got back home
he'll be back to retaliate!

no he won't said the man
eating his pancakes and eggs

those guys, those neighborhood legends
still wore their afros, black jackets, and medallions

Portrait of a Father: 2014.

Say Hello to my faggot kid
is how Ed's dad
started introducing him
to the buddies who would
drink in the garage with him
after their Wednesday softball games
if Ed ever ran into them.
Bye faggot kid
he would wave when Ed would leave
all because the he'd started wearing skinny jeans.

Party Hats

I'm in a taxi when I see them.
Every member of our Department
but me. The Black. In their cardboard cone
party hats. Tumbling out of Pete's restaurant.
Laughing at God knows what.

IV.

Fisherman's Cap

One reed-thin fisher
and his daughter.
One boat. One net. Many small
conversations.
Over coffee
when they break
on the sea.

At a Seaside Restaurant in Maine

Dad must've had a stroke or something, because the dark-haired daughter kept snapping his picture with her camera phone, saying, "Dad, you look *so* majestic." And the lighter-haired daughter sat her daughter down on his lap and said, "See Daddy? You can totally still hold her."

She got the toddler's attention: "Abby. Abbs, sweetheart. Look! Isn't Grandpa Henry strong?" She made a muscle to indicate how strong. Then the dark-haired son with his sunglasses still on inside said to Abby, "Fuck yeah he's strong." At that, Dad got emotional. His poor wife wiped his mouth.

soles with holes

because bible-believing folks
kick out their abomination
kids,
forty percent of our nation's
homeless
are teens
and inbetweens.

an inbetween is one who's not quite
adolescent, but not quite teen. so, like,
eleven.

Hospital Gown

If you want to know
who your friends are
get sick

Adult Diapers

When you read about alcohol abuse you may think of college campuses and Spring Break, but there's another demographic that is seriously affected by alcoholism: the elderly.

—*Six Facts About Elderly Alcohol Abuse*

Aunt Song didn't get bit till she was seventy.
Seven Zero.
Let that sink in.
We come home
and she's have peed
in the foyer or refrigerator door.
Mopping up, she points and laughs at us,
and calls us little pissants.
Aunt Song, I swear, has never said
a cuss word in her life.
Do word searches, clean, and cook for us
was all she'd ever want in her life, we thought.
Now when we take off her diaper, to wipe
between her legs if she's pissed herself,
she'll call us emeffing nutcrackers,
little pissants,
mama's boys
or worse.

V.

poem for autumn

come wind,
rain,
short days to watch from windows.
come indian summer sunny afternoons.

come cheeseburger tailgate.
come wearing your nebraska red
husker football go team! gear.

come season of sweaters and boots;
season of hot apple cider with cinnamon;

coffee and kahlua saturday mornings;
come have a cup.

come on, september! c'mon!
you brown microfiber blanket,
you wild and crazy red and orange
chocolate yellow thing.
come cuddles on the sofa with the cat.

the hawk is out

wind around us rattles the   windows   like a demon
shaking the shoulders of a soul seller

the sound his jangling teeth make the sound the windowpanes make

                         it's the hawk out there

                         going to get in   like a thief   a rent
collector

                                  pregnant possum   circling this home

climbing on top   dropping the temperature inside and
everywhere   candle wicks

stay lit although   barely   even carpeted floors requires
socks

                         shoe-bottomed slippers   and worried
attention.   all

around us the hawk   his teeth and muscles.

Living Alone in Nebraska

It's pretty
Difficult to be sad
Outside
In glorious Nebraska
Autumn
On the balcony of your apartment
A chenille Cornhusker blanket
On your bare legs
You are wearing a little robe
Writing
The dog's sitting near
Captivated at squirrels
Dumpster-diving
Coming up with ketchup'd fries
One of them found a tub of hummus
Due to your allergies you
Smell little
But you can feel now
Your loneliness
Will pass
As seasons always
Have.

ebony

in the hallway, it's all butters and browns
the sun through the manila shades of
the rectangle windows sheen everything
everything made of good wood
like it used to be
when men worked with their hands
wood cut, carried, buffed, sanded
when men worked with their hands
they built fine, fine things
they worked in the morning through
the heat of the day here
a woman with black hair and blue jeans
sitting on these sunlit stairs
waiting, i believe for someone
or just enjoying the wood

VI.

The Nike Song Circa '91

Public Ridicule:
Grade school crush: Mike.
That Michael Jackson song
The Way You Make Me Feel.
Michael Jackson said:
Pretty baby with the high heels on,
you give me fever like I've never known.

I sang it to MikeMike—what we called him.
I improvised:
Pretty baby with the Nikes on.
We were in his backyard
before the boys came to play ball.
He laughed and said I sounded like a chicken.

And he told everyone
about my/our song.

The Day I Left the Church

"you will be too much for some people.
those are not your people. "
—anon

I looked around and something occurred to me. Every woman there was
no woman I wanted to be, ever. They were burlap sacks. Skirts longer
than Sundays and fat. Thirsty for a word: Blessed are the Poor in Spirit.
But I ain't poor. I looked around and something occurred to me. No
woman there was any woman I wanted to be ever. They kept asking me
to do things I didn't feel like doing: Turn to your neighbor and say this.
Shake somebody's hand and say that. Give me 10 percent of your bread.
Shuck. Jive. Hell naw. No woman there was any woman I wanted to be.
One day, a lady said to me, "Sister Christian…" But I wasn't listening. I
was thinking, Don't call me sister. I am *not* related to y'all. At all. All of
y'all here asking God to send you a man. Sista, I ain't gotta pray to get
a brotha. I ain't like y'all. Me and my peeps, see, we wear more jewelry
than clothes. We wear diamond studs in our noses. Our lovers (or y'all's)
polish our toes. They rub our thighs with almond oil till they glow. We
wear fishnet hose so we show through the holes. Y'all all wearing the
wrong color hose. And shoes that look like y'all men's.

on robes

i *knew* never to take
something of value.
still, i got home,
got unpacked,
and goddamit i left my
favorite pink robe
on the bathroom hook
of the tokyo hilton.
my husband had given
me that robe after
one of my miscarriages.
he'd said check, make sure
you didn't leave anything.
but i didn't check because
i was checking facebook.

The Professor Takes His Lunch

A professor is seated on the fire escape
Of an apartment in an historic neighborhood
Of famous architecture homes
With copper gargoyles or nymphs or wondrous oddities
Gone green. The smell of corner laundry facility
Fabric softener floats up to him. He closes his eyes and breathes
It in.
It's Riverside Drive. It is now eleven-forty
And he puts down his students' short stories.
The fifty-something professor sits daydreaming for
Semester's end before getting to his sandwich
With heavy mayonnaise and shredded chicken. He
Has on jeans and tennis shoes but is a professional above
The waist; reading glasses and a smart cap.
He sits left ankle over right knee, forms a leg table.
His lady is here.
His head and neck now crane left to see where she reads,
Nods off, in his bed.
He puts his right hand to his chest, in love, and then
Slowly strokes his chin hairs into a V, what he does
When he is thinking of her. He saves her half
His sandwich. He removes the smart cap, places it on his face,
Uncrosses his legs and leans back to fantasize. Meanwhile,
Above him, the clouds are thinning, showing the sun
The day warms him up
Up there on the flower-potted
Fire escape, on top of the world.

Biological Father at College Graduation, 2001

Angelo shows up at the 11 am ceremony smelling like a liquor store floor. Wearing a swishy jogging suit from the 90s, a pinky ring and plastic gas station sunglasses. He'd gotten a ticket somehow.

He hadn't been to bed; he'd been to the casino. And to women's. I knew it. I'd seen it on him many a time. He handed me the ten hundred dollar bills he'd won. I took it and rolled my eyes.

At lunch at Good Time Charley's that afternoon, he brought a prostitute date. She looked just like a prostitute too—didn't even have coochie hair I could tell—that's how tight her lil bubblegum pink dress was.

The two of them drank 11 Coors and 8 margaritas. But he paid for all 50 of my family and friends, and stuffed another hundred in my hand. I still don't know who ratted me out and told him Good Time Charley's.

VII.

Portrait of a Medicine Man

On a hot November day when everyone is out marveling that the sun is
too, I spot this kid with half a dozen older men outside the bodega. I can
see he is delivering them drugs.

Joints rolled skinny in white papers slipped in plaid front pockets slid in
palms stuck in back pockets of belted Dickies.
The kid sees me.

He comes over to where I'm seated on the stoop. He says, Just so you
know, Ma, I ain't no drug dealer or nothin. I be giving them that because
they be needin it.

I'm gon be a barber. Aks anybody. I'm in barber school now.
He kid pulls off his hoodie to show me his head. It's Nipsey.
It's fire! I tell him so. He says, I know.

House Guest Who Stole My Wedding Ring

Shame
She'd have grown
far richer
as my friend

portrait of pink, or blush

when today at a bistro
an elderly couple in jeans, leather
bomber jackets and heeled boots
stepped down from their stools
to stand and go home –

him behind her,
his bomber jacket zipper
a spine at her back,
him wrapping in her scarf

the heart-shaped cookie she nibbled
the shape of her mouth,
that cookie, puffy,
with still-soft icing white and rose –

I learned

the anthropology of blush

The Butcher's Apron: A Portrait of Whole Foods,

or,

Harlem Gentrification

The old Kenyan
makes a living
slaughtering goats.

Not for curry goat, for
Manhattaners'
dogs.

Portrait of Debra

I remember we didn't have raincoats. We didn't have umbrellas either. It was raining like hell. Debra'd asked me to go down to The Avenue of the Americas with her, where there was the Citibank. My job was to cameraphonephotograph her walking casually in front of the bank. And then the following would/could happen: I'd text her the pics. She'd be lovely with wet hair and noirsexy with her mascara running. She'd edit with cropping and filters if needed. Then she'd post, *In Manhattan with my favorite girlfriend!!* and tag me @Adrienne. Donovan Johnson would be active on Facebook. He'd "like" and write something like, *Citibank! Yo! That's where I work.* To which I'd comment, *Come and holla at ya girls! (three pink hearts emoji)* He'd arrive and I'd have to go make some urgent phone call, after having footsied him under the table, after having kept touching his thigh—laying his napkin in his lap, feeling out the texture of his pants. The two of them alone, Debra'd mention it was probably my boyfriend on the call. Donnie'd say something like, *Oh, her profile says she's single.* She'd say, *She forgot to update it.* And, already slightly turned on, already slightly drunk, he'd be fine with the next best thing/ girl. So, Debra would start footsying. I thought the whole idea was *insane.* I gave her all of my spiels about esteem and not chasing a man, letting him chase her. *Don't get with the man that* you *want; get with the man that wants* you. But she fired back, *Everybody ain't a unicorn like you, Adrienne. Some girls gotta get the leftovers. It ain't desperate; it's life.* No, we shouldn't've been plotting like this; but, you don't know Donovan Johnson. Blue-eyed black man. Timberlands. Yankee fitted cap. Bought already-faded light blue True Religion jeans. Tattoo he did himself. The infamous Graffiti Kid growing up in Queens. Bad boy turned Investment Banker *Boss.* When he met us at Citibank he was suited though it was Saturday, because he'd met with a client on his way over. But when he came to hang out with us at my place later that night, he was no longer Manhattan. He was Cool J Queens. He did me first. Then, still turned on, still tipsy, did Debra. Right away Debra got pregnant. Donovan married her then. The three of us are still friends.

VIII.

The Ad Agency Workers

No one wants to be here
in boxed-in solitude.
We won't make art, we fear—
creative flow subdued.

In boxed-in solitude,
we wait here for our tasks.
Creative flow subdued,
we do just what Boss asks.

We wait here for our tasks—
the same ones as last year.
We do just what Boss asks;
why even keep us here?

The same year after year—
because this model worked.
To it we must adhere
in khakis and blue shirts.

The Guy in the Office Next to Mine

I could say, Hey
You going
To the reading this Thursday?
I'll come if you come.
Or I could get dressed up
In something
With an impossible-to-reach back zipper,
And pretty-plead for some assistance.

I could wait for the rainy season.
Then be always ready to leave
When he's always ready to leave
And offer to give him a ride.
Or I could offer him my
Perfumed wrists and ask please
For some bracelet latch
Assistance.

And then, one day, I could not knock.
Just sit and sip my tea, and read
News.
But I'd have strategically placed my necklace
On my desk
Having it serve as a
Conversation
Piece.

He'd walk by and say,
Don't you need my help today?
Your help?? I'd say.
With your necklace, he'd point.
Need help putting it on?
Oh that! Well, that's called a
Choker. But, sure, you can do that.
Please and thank you.

Poem for my PhD Professor

I like your Facebook pics.
I pray for staff meetings when
I get to hear you say something—
anything.
Curse spring break and MLK Day—
days without you.
Miss you wearing that cowl neck sweater,
those slacks where I see your print.
Your cologne. I dream us kissing
pressed against our office walls—
yours again,
or maybe mine next time.

Cutting One's Lover's Hair

I want to touch my lover but he's gone and cut his beard. I am stunned.
I am blinking back tears. He talks and I try to look at him. Try. Imagine
Santa with no beard, a lion without his. Looking all skinny and weird,
and like a chick. Imagine loving a woman for her hair. Imagine you
head to the bar after work with your work friends. And you invite
your stunning model-look-alike woman. And she shows us bald af,
embarrassing you. You who's been bragging about your model-look-alike
woman. With her hair, before, when you introduced her to people they'd
gasp. And you just loved it. With this new hairstyle now you want to
rush a plastic bag over her head, and get her out of there before your
friends see her. Or rush a plastic bag over her head and just kill. For
cutting off your hair.

Armchair

The armrest of her armchair is wearing her
red Target work shirt and khakis. And her earrings
that look pretty but grow heavy. The back of
the armchair is wearing her polkadot bra, the
carpet in front of the chair, her socks and draws.

It is positioned in front of her electric fireplace just below
her wall-mounted flat screen. She comes home and sits
to read but falls asleep, and wakes at around threeish,
always because she's gotten too hot.
She stands, goes pee, wonders if she should climb in bed,
but after work she really needs that artificial fire. So it's back to
the chair—
she peels off the clothes she's sweated through.
Lays them on their spots.

IX.

Walgreen's Run

Only on Halloween does she miss homeownership.
She is ordinary tonight, not
The Lady Who Gives Whole Snickers and
Silver Dollars.
Not The Good Witch Lady wearing the tiara.

When her lover sees she's almost in tears about this,
really missing those kids,
her house,
he says, C'mon. Let's go get Twix for dessert.
He winks, It'll be my treat.

Before the walk to Walgreen's,
he raids the center console of his car
for change—
for her.

winter windows

bakeries, boutiques, and other places, all with frosted windows.

biting off his right-hand glove he writes my name in a heart with
his nail. he

breaks off an icicle we share like a popsicle, as we make our way down

broadway. our hands in each other's

back pockets.

dancing with him,

or

my baby's back muscles

have him hold you
and you'll never have another man
hold you again. they will all be boys
compared.

have him walk you to the dance floor
spin you once then pull you close
whisper to you
his cinnamon altoids breath

what's he telling you, girl
i'd fight a polar bear
with fish in my pockets every night
for you.

watch him grin at you like
you're a pie, you're a paycheck
have him rock you all night
and still feel steady

Balls Smell

Girls, do you too love balls smell?
Because I'm *in l o v e* with my husband's balls smell.

Here we are sitting on the sofa. I've got my head in his lap.
He's got on nothing but his draws. That balls smell.

Thinking about it I shudder like a feather on the ear. I love his cologne
too. But I really love his balls smell.

We're watching Harlem Nights or whatever. Friday night. He's drinking
Heineken. I'm drinking in that balls smell.

These Boss black boxer briefs I stuffed in his stocking for Christmas.
Right now I'm about to stuff these giant balls

in my mouth,
teabag these awesome balls.

I won't take off his draws. I love these draws. I'll just pull them to the
side. Just enjoy the balls.

Right now he tryna fuck. But all I want is this right now.
I tell him, Pour some Heineken on em. Mmm balls.

tittyfucking after the miscarriage

we do it on the floor.
his belt binding my boobs.

i do it to have use for them
now.

Notes and Acknowledgments

"Soles with Holes" takes its inspiration from the March 29. 2017 *Washington Post* article titled, "Homeless rates for LGBT teens are alarming, but parents can make a difference" by Jaimie Seaton. Most notably the following selection:

"Up to 1.6 million young people experience homelessness in the United States every year. Forty percent of them identify as LGBT (lesbian, gay, bisexual or transgender), according to a 2012 study conducted by the Williams Institute at UCLA Law. It's estimated that LGBT youth represent about 7 percent of the population, which puts that 40 percent figure into heartbreaking context.

"The study's other findings are equally bleak: 46 percent of homeless LGBT youths ran away because of family rejection of their sexual orientation or gender identity; 43 percent were forced out by parents, and 32 percent faced physical, emotional or sexual abuse at home.

""There are several reasons parents reject their LGBT youth," said Telaina Eriksen, author of "Unconditional: A Guide to Loving and Supporting Your LGBTQ Child." "Sometimes it is based on religion; they think that their child is a sinner or that their child needs to be punished so they see 'the error of their ways.' They might think if they force their child to leave their home, their child may return repenting, magically somehow no longer LGBT."

Thank you to the readers and editors of the following publications for publishing selected poems:

"Wedding Dress." *Common Ground Review* (2020). Print.

"The Day I Left the Church." *Connecticut River Review* (2020) Print.

"Lincoln." *Conclave* (2020). Online.

"Soles with Holes." *Conclave* (2020). Online.

"The Professor Takes His Lunch." *Typishly* (2020). Online.

"The Hawk is Out." *Imspired* (2020). Online.

"Living Alone in Nebraska." *Imspired* (2020). Online.

"Portrait of Debra." *Hayden's Ferry* (2020). Print.

"Armchair." *Marble Poetry* (2020). Online.

"Portrait of Pink." *All the Songs We Sing* (2020). Print.

"The Guy in the Office Next Door to Mine." *Cliterature* (2018). Online.

"The Butcher's Apron *or* Harlem Gentrification." *Radix Media* (2018). 128. Print.

"Tittyfucking After the Miscarriage." *Cliterature* (2017). Online.
"Walgreen's Run." *Concis* (2016). Online.

"The Ad Agency Workers." *Obsidian* (2016). Print.

Thank you to Andrew Gifford and the staff at Santa Fe Writers Project.

Thank you to my University of Nebraska-Lincoln family, especially Kwame Dawes, Ted Kooser, Stacey Waite, Jeannette Eileen Jones, and Kwakiutl Dreher, who worked with me on these poems. Thank you, Timothy Schaffert, Chigozie Obioma, Joy Castro, William Thomas, and Marco Abel for going above and beyond. Thank you, Kate Pierson, Rachel Cochran, Maria Nazos, Hope Wabuke, Matthew Guzman, and Fran Kaye.

Lenard D. Moore and L. Teresa Church of The Carolina African-American Writers Collective, thank you for being my poetry parents. Thank you, Crystal Simone Smith.

Cornelius Eady and Toi Derricotte, thank you for Cave Canem. Thank you, Furious Flower. Thank you, Blue Ridge Mountains Collective.

Reeko Nathaniel and Natira Yates, thank you for reminding me poetry is important, and for being my biggest fans.

Michael Hayes, Rasheda Williams, Vincent Chandler, Tamika Thompson, Claudia Zonca, Vern Sanders, thank you for being family and friends.

Thank you to the Robinson family, the Kelley family, the Hendrix family, the Stewart family, the James family, and the Christian family. Thank you especially, Mark Christian, for your incredible support.

About the Author

Adrienne Christian is a poet, writer, and fine art photographer. Her work has appeared in *Prairie Schooner*, *Hayden's Ferry Review*, *CALYX*, *phoebe*, *The Los Angeles Review* as The Editor's Choice, and elsewhere. She is the author of two previous poetry collections, *A Proper Lover* and *12023 Woodmont Avenue*. A fellow of both Cave Canem and Callaloo writing residencies, she earned her B.A. from The University of Michigan, her M.F.A. from Pacific University, and her PhD from the University of Nebraska.

Find her at adriennechristian.com